soup in season

soup in season

soups from the Regent kitchen
(& Hunterston Farm delectables)

Tom Wuest, Karen Hollenbeck Wuest
& Peter La Grand

with original linocuts by Peter La Grand

R
Regent College Publishing

Soup in Season: Soups from the Regent Kitchen and Hunterston Farm Delectables
Copyright © 2019 by Tom Wuest, Karen Hollenbeck Wuest, and Peter La Grand

Originally published in 2005 by Happy Chicken Press

This revised edition published 2019 by
Regent College Publishing
5800 University Boulevard
Vancouver, BC V6T 2E4 Canada

All rights reserved. No part of this publication may be reproduced, stored in a retrieval system, or transmitted, in any form or by any means, electronic, mechanical, photocopying, recording or otherwise, without the prior written permission of the author, except in the case of brief quotations embodied in critical articles and reviews.

Regent College Publishing is an imprint of the Regent Bookstore <www.regentbookstore.com>. Views expressed in works published by Regent College Publishing are those of the author and do not necessarily represent the official position of Regent College <www.regent-college.edu>.

ISBN 978-1-57383-579-4

Contents

Foreword to the Revised Edition   1
Acknowledgments   3
From the Original Introduction   4
Sharing the Table   5
To the Soup Eaters at Regent College   7
Cooking for Crowds   8
Abbreviations, Glossary & Some Basics   11

Beans
     Brazilian Black Bean   16
     Black Bean (variations)   17
     Louisiana Red Beans with Rice   18
     Tuscan White Bean with Rosemary   19
     White Bean (variations)   20

Legumes
     Arkansas Black-eyed Pea   22
     Moroccan Harira (Chickpea)   23
     Spicy Mexican Lentil, Chile & Roasted Garlic   25
     Lentil (variations)   25
     Swedish Split Pea   27
     Split Pea (variations)   27
     Thai-Vietnamese Fusion: Peanut Phô   28
     Spicy West African Peanut   30

Chilies
     New Mexican Chili Potato   32

Leeks
     Potato Leek   34

Potatoes
     Monastic Cheese and Potato   36

Corn
     Summer Corn, Zucchini & Chili Chowder   39

Mushrooms
     Tomato Mushroom Bisque   42
     Asian Wild Mushroom & Leek   44

Winter Squash
     Thanksgiving Pumpkin Apple Curry   46
     Hunterston Farm Squash with Orange & Ginger   48
     Indonesian Coconut Curry Squash   49

The Garden
     Summer Minestrone   52
     Winter Minestrone   53

A Weekend around the Wilkinson's Table   56

Foreword to the Revised Edition

Fifteen years since self-publishing this small collection of soup recipes, we are now turning this cookbook over to Regent Publishing. We are deeply grateful to Bill Reimer and Caroline Ahn for bringing it back into print!

Much, of course, has changed since we collaborated on this project in 2005. However, we still prepare these soups in much the same way today as we did on those long-ago Tuesdays at Regent, and so we have not changed the recipes much, if at all.

Karen and I now have two teenage sons, and Peter is married and has three children. The three of us no longer live in the Commercial Drive neighborhood of East Vancouver, and most of the stores we mention in "Sharing the Table" are no longer in business. The house we shared on East First Avenue has been torn down, and the old-world gardens, grapevine, and fruit trees we tended have been covered with concrete. Isaiah no longer eats fistfuls of dirt from the garden. We have also become much better cooks, since we have devoted a large portion of every day over the past decades to feeding our children good food.

Along with these changes, we have witnessed a growing awareness about the connections between healthy food and healthy societies, between clean air, water, and soil and healthy human bodies, the health of creation, and the health of the whole world. More people recognize that we are all suffering from the short-sighted pursuit of profit, that we have taken more than we need from the creation, and that we are upsetting the God-made balance of all things. A continual stream of wayfarers who are seeking a vision of the world whole and healed are finding their way to this hillside farm, proclaiming with their lives and longings, "The earth is the Lord's and all that dwell therein" (Ps 24:1).

In our own story, we have moved from Vancouver to Galiano Island to the lush and lonely hills of the Brush Creek valley in southern Ohio. We are tasting and seeing the goodness of God in this particular ecology, having left industrial food behind in search of the "headwaters," or ancient traditions, of hand-cultivation and the building of healthy communities one person, one creature, one species at a time. The calcium-rich "sweet" water in our soup stock comes from limestone springs on the farm. The dairy we add to our soups begins in lush green pastures and is transformed through spring and summer rains, the miracle of photosynthesis, and the labor of hand-milking into cream and, with time and bacterial energy, hard cheese.

Here in rural America, on the edge of Appalachia, we cannot access many of the ingredients mentioned in these pages—Middle Eastern spices, dried Chinese mushrooms, fresh ginger, Asian noodles. Thus we have taken to improvising, relying entirely on what is in season, and foraging often. What a gift to head up the hill behind our house into the woodland, the canopy alight with budding tulip poplars and maples, on a warm April morning to search for morels, ramps, and wild garlic for a spring cream soup—or to pluck wood ear mushrooms from a rotting log while gathering firewood and then string them over the wood stove to dry so we can make a healing pot of midwinter phô. In mid-September, visitors might find themselves feasting on late-summer garden ratatouille over creamy polenta made from field corn grown in this watershed and ground at our neighbor's grist mill. Towards the end of autumn, we might be eating *pasta e fagioli* (rustic pasta, bean, and vegetable soup) stewed with fresh squirrel from our neighbors.

May the soups in this book spark your curiosity towards the relationships between all things. May they inspire you to seek the one who imagined and created salt and cayenne pepper, onions and garlic, basil and rosemary with love and joy. May you be abundantly nourished by the one who fashioned potatoes and leeks, black beans and jalapeños, tomatoes and eggplant, fish and cream, bread and wine. May every meal be a reminder of the loving feast Christ prepared for his disciples on the shores of Galilee.

Should you ever find yourselves passing through southeastern Ohio, about six miles upstream from the confluence of Ohio Brush Creek and the Ohio River, you are welcome to *come and eat* and to *taste and see* the good gifts of God that are in season at our table throughout the year.

–Tom, Karen, Isaiah & Arbutus
Isidore's Plough on Brush Creek, Adams County, Ohio
March 2019

Acknowledgements

We culled these recipes from many sources and then adapted them for Soup Group at Regent. Following are some of the cookbooks we liked best: *Twelve Months of Monastery Soups* by Brother Victor-Antoine d'Avila-Latourrette, *Soup and Bread: A Country Inn Cookbook* by Crescent Dragonwagon, *Sundays at Moosewood Restaurant: Ethnic and Regional Recipes* by the Moosewood Collective, and *Fields of Greens* by Annie Somerville. We have also gleaned from *Chez Panisse Vegetables* by Alice Waters. The recipe for the Vietnamese phô came from experiments in our home kitchen and a conversation with folks at The Mekong on Commercial Drive.

Thanks to Ralph at Eternal Abundance on Commercial Drive for his commitment to fill his humble storefront with beautiful, organically grown (and, whenever possible, locally grown) produce—and for his generosity in giving us a significant discount on that produce every week. Walking through his sparse storefront and hand-selecting vegetables with my son, Isaiah, every Monday afternoon was one of the highlights of my week.

Special thanks to Loren & Mary Ruth Wilkinson for providing us with fifty pounds of Hunterston Farm butternut squash for the roasted butternut squash soup we made for Thanksgiving—and for the recipes they pulled together so we could include them at the end of this book.

Many thanks to all who helped chop onions, mince garlic, dice carrots, cube potatoes, slice buns, serve soup, wash dishes and mop the floor in faithful service to Regent students and faculty week after week. We enjoyed working alongside you.

Finally, our heartfelt gratitude to Carrie Herbert, whose gracious gift of service, seasoned experience in the kitchen, company, and conversation we enjoyed each Tuesday throughout the year.

From the Original Introduction

The soups in this book have been prepared for crowds of 250–300. While all of them have also been tested in our household kitchen at some point in the past two years, they are still only approximations. We encourage you to use them as templates rather than prescriptions. We hope you will experiment, substitute and season to suit your own tastes.

Whether you're cooking from this recipe book or another one, we hope you won't waste time running from store to store looking for a particular ingredient—nor money buying a specialty item you most likely won't ever use again. Experiment, make substitutions and keep tasting, trusting the palate God gave you.

The book ends with a sampling of recipes from Mary Ruth and Loren Wilkinson—a most appropriate conclusion, since they are the ones who actually began the community Soup Group meal way back when they first came to Regent. (And they were the first soup chefs!) Anyone who's sat around their table on a rainy winter morning eating waffles buried with homemade raspberry syrup and whipped cream, or enjoyed a sunrise on the back deck with a mug of hot coffee and a cinnamon roll, or picked basil in their garden for a fresh pesto pasta candlelight feast will be delighted to have these recipes at hand.

Sharing the Table

Every Tuesday, from September through April, we gather in the atrium to share a simple meal of soup and bread, a continuation of our chapel communion. As we eat, we remember that the gifts that sustain us come from God's creation. Sharing the table with one another, we live the gospel, weaving the biblical stories that have shaped us into our own stories—the rich abundance of the Garden of Eden, the Passover meal, manna raining down from heaven, a wedding feast, the fish and the loaves, the Last Supper, the Resurrection Day fish breakfast, the Eucharist, and a foreshadowing of the marriage supper of the Lamb, the feast day of celebration and fellowship that will never cease.

As we gather around tables, we listen to stories of joy and sorrow, and we help one another along the way. As we engage with people from around the world, we particularize our sense of belonging to a global human family. The solitary are brought into families (Psalm 68), and we become a richer and fuller reflection of the universal body of Christ.

The pre-packaged, artificially flavored, chemically stabilized, genetically modified food that many of us eat today is produced in distant factories or grown in far-flung fields by a shrinking number of corporations, many of which depend upon the resources and cheap labor of the two-thirds world. We have chosen convenient and quick over a commitment to thoughtful relationship with the creation through gardening and husbandry. The breakdown of the family parallels the forgoing of table fellowship in American culture. Our consumption of food (or, for those of us with eating disorders, our rejection of food) has become less about nourishment and more about satisfying cravings, controlling our nerves and battling fatigue, depression and the mediated images we carry of the human body. When the food we eat is merely shaken out of boxes, dumped out of cans, pulled from the microwave, rattled out of machines or consumed out of paper sacks while driving alone along congested streets, then the meal ceases to be a sacrament, a feast of nourishment, a gift to the stranger, a prophetic witness to our neighbors.

As our contemporary culture becomes "more and more artificial, less and less human" (Romano Guardini), our table fellowship can become prophetic witness.

In preparing the soup meal for Regent each week, we have intentionally thought about how we can foster both faithful stewardship of the creation and community. The fresh herbs for the soups have all come from my backyard urban garden on East First Avenue. Whenever possible, I hand-selected ingredients from independent markets in my neighborhood on Commercial Drive—primarily Eternal Abundance, an independent organic produce market; Santa Barbara, a Portuguese market with a wonderful array of cheeses and European specialty items; and El Sureno, a bulk food Indian market specializing in Mexican and Indian items. The Portuguese buns are baked in the early morning hours each Tuesday at Strawberry Bakery, a Hungarian bakery three blocks from my house. I have nurtured relationships with all of these shopkeepers not only because of my weekly shopping for Regent, but because these are the markets where Peter, Karen and I buy food for our household.

More and more, I have been thinking about making soups that reflect the season—eating seasonally supports area farms and also ensures that we are eating food as God created it to be eaten, in the season God intended for us to enjoy it.

You water the hills from your upper chambers;
The earth is satisfied with the fruit of your works.
You cause the grass to grow for the cattle,
And vegetation for the service of all,
That we may bring forth food from the earth,
And wine that makes glad our hearts,
Oil to make our faces shine,
And bread which strengthens our hearts.

These all wait for you,
That you may give them their food in due season.
What you give them they gather in;
You open your hand, they are filled with good.
—Psalm 104:13–15, 27–28

Though it's crowded and often rushed, though you have to wait in line and typically sit on the floor, our weekly meals are feasts, when we gather to celebrate the goodness of God's gifts to us in our daily bread and in the gift of Jesus, who has reconciled us to God and to one another.

We have designed this book with the hope that it will help you extend the table fellowship that you have received at Regent to all you meet in the places where you live, work, play and pray. May you "…plant vineyards and drink wine from them…make gardens and eat fruit from them…" (Amos 9:14), and may you extend to all Christ's invitation to "Come and eat…" (John 21:12).

Live well—
the household of
Tom, Karen, Isaiah
& Peter

To the Soup Eaters at Regent College

Brothers and sisters—
I, Tom Wuest,
And I, Peter La Grand,
Will be making soup for you this year
And we want to take this chance to formally
And humbly
Apologize in advance for all the times when
    the soup is late
    the soup is early
    the soup is undercooked
    the soup is overcooked
    the soup is too hot
    the soup is too cold
    the soup is burned
    the soup is mislabeled
    the soup is unedible, or
        when there is no bread
        when we run out of butter
        when there is no meat soup
        when the sour cream runs dry
        when the salsa is too hot
        when the salsa is not hot enough
        when your child will not eat the soup
        when the soup is not Kraft Dinner
        when the line is too long
        when the peanut butter has jam in it
        when the jam has peanut butter in it
        when we run out of bowls
            or spoons
            or cups
            or patience
Forgive us,
we humbly ask,
and when we ignore
    or mistreat
    or abuse in any way you as patrons or volunteers
when we choose to make soup that brings back painful
    childhood memories
when we are quick to speak and quick to anger
when we rant about uneaten food or about dishes
ecological
agricultural
    hypothetical
    theoretical or
        theological rants about the state of our
        world,
    forgive us and know that we, your soup
makers, are doing the best that we can,
but that we, like you, are only human.

Cooking for Crowds

We thought others who cook for crowds might be interested in knowing about how much it takes to prepare soup for 250–300—and we also wanted to pass along some of the tips we've discovered along the way for cooking large volumes. (It doesn't really work all that well to simply multiply a recipe intended to feed 6–8 people by 50.)

Guide for Increasing Measurements

Salt: Never multiply the salt out for a large recipe. Learn to salt early in the cooking process. (We always add salt and pepper to the each batch of sauté and a bit more when we combine all the ingredients in the soup pot.) Too much salt added at the end gives a raw salt taste. However, soups and sauces should always be *lightly* salted, because the salt gets stronger as the liquid reduces in the simmering process. Think of salt as a flavor enhancer—not something you should taste on its own.

As a rough guide, for a 10-gallon pot of soup, I might use around 3 T of salt. In general, soups that have a lot of potatoes (or pasta or rice) need more salt. If it's toward the end of cooking time and you're desperate for more salt, add soy sauce instead of salt—the liquid form will be more readily absorbed and you'll avoid the raw salt flavor.

Seasoning: Never double, triple, etc. When cooking for 25–30, you might end up using half the regular amount. But for larger quantities, you'll end up cutting the seasoning by a third—or even more. Add seasoning slowly through the various stages of the cooking process, tasting a few minutes after each addition. When you "roast" the spices by adding them to the sauté—as we suggest in all of the recipes—you infuse the garlic, onions and other vegetables with the rich flavors, while also encouraging the spices to release their oils.) Don't add a bunch of seasoning at the end—all seasonings, like salt, need to "cook" into the soup by simmering for at least 3–5 minutes. Otherwise, they will add a raw or chalky flavor to the soup.

Sweetener: You don't need to increase the small amount used to enhance flavor (i.e., to sweeten carrots or squash that aren't sweet enough) or to cut acidity (i.e., when using canned tomatoes) by very much. For instance, I might use only about 1 t of honey per gallon of tomato-based soup (or about 1 c of honey for 25 gallons).

Fat: When expanding a recipe, you'll only use about 1/4 (or less) of the butter or oil. For instance, if a single recipe that serves 6–8 people calls for 2 T of olive oil, you won't need to use 6.25 cups to serve 300 (thank goodness!). Instead, you'll probably use about 1–1.5 cups.

Basic Minestrone

makes 25 gallons; serves 250–300

13–16 gallons water
15 bay leaves
lots of fresh rosemary sprigs
8 # dried chickpeas (sorted & soaked overnight)
15 # potatoes (scrubbed & cut into 1/2" cubes)
8–10 # carrots (scrubbed & cut
 in half lengthwise, then
 sliced crosswise)
8–10 # celery (sliced crosswise)
15 bell peppers, assorted colors
 (seeds & stem removed,
 then diced)
10 medium zucchini (unpeeled,
 quartered lengthwise,
 & sliced crosswise)
30–40 yellow onions (peeled & chopped)
10–15 heads garlic (peeled & minced)
1/3–1/2 c dried leaf basil
1/3–1/2 c dried leaf oregano
1/4–1/3 c dried thyme
1 bottle dry red or white wine
8–10 bunches spinach (washed, trimmed & sliced into
 1/2" ribbons)
5 100-oz cans diced tomatoes
1 100-oz can crushed tomatoes
1 28-oz can tomato paste
1 c honey
6 # pasta (any small shape)
5 bunches fresh basil (washed, stemmed & sliced into
 thin ribbons)
2–3 # spiced green pitted olives (sliced)
salt & pepper to taste

Garnishes
5 # grated Parmesan cheese
6–8 bunches Italian parsley (washed, stemmed & chopped)
30 dozen Portuguese buns
5 # butter

Divide about 13 gallons of fresh water between soup pots (you'll need 25 gallons total volume) and place on burners. Divide soaked, drained chickpeas between the pots, along with bay leaves and fresh rosemary sprigs. Bring to a boil over high heat.

As you finish chopping each vegetable, divide it among your soup pots. (Add potatoes first, then carrots, then celery and finally bell peppers.) When water is at a rolling boil, reduce heat a bit and let the soup continue to simmer. (*Note:* due to the large volume of water, you cannot turn the heat down too low, or the chickpeas and vegetables will not cook—but neither do you want the soup boiling away like mad.)

When cooking for crowds, you'll need to stand guard over the soup pots, stirring almost constantly—particularly with heavy soups that are liable to stick and burn.

While vegetables are cooking, heat olive oil over medium heat in large, heavy pan. Sauté the onion in batches, making sure that you don't overcrowd the pan (thereby "boiling" the onions rather than sautéing them). Add some salt and pepper to each batch and sauté until the onion is soft. Add some garlic, a little of each herb (basil, oregano and thyme) and continue to sauté for a few more minutes. Then add a few splashes of the red or white wine and sauté until the liquid has been absorbed.

Transfer each batch of sauté to a bowl as you finish it, deglazing the sauté pan with another splash of wine. (If the chickpeas are tender when you finish the first batch of sauté, you can go ahead and add the sauté directly to the soup pot, but if they're not, the salt in the sauté will make the skins toughen—and retard the cooking process.)

When the chickpeas are tender, add all the sauté, the tomatoes, tomato paste and honey, along with the zucchini. (You don't want to add the tomatoes before the chickpeas are tender, because the acid in the tomatoes may make the skins toughen—and retard the cooking process.)

As the vegetables continue to cook, taste and adjust seasonings in each pot, stirring to keep the chickpeas and heavy vegetables from sinking to the bottom of the pot and burning. (Add more honey if tomatoes are too acidic; add more salt and pepper, if necessary.)

Roughly 15 minutes before serving, divide the pasta among the soup pots.

Thin with additional water and/or tomato purée if necessary.

Roughly 5 minutes before serving, add the spinach ribbons and the sliced green olives.

Add the (optional) basil ribbons just before serving.

Though this recipe is a rough guide for making a minestrone that will serve about 250–300 people, the process for making a large volume of any of the soups in this book is similar.

For roughly 25 gallons of soup, I almost *always* use the following:

13–16 gallons water
15 bay leaves
8–10 # carrots
8–10 # celery

I make up the remaining volume with beans or legumes, tomatoes, a variety of other vegetables (squash, potatoes, mushrooms, bell peppers, spinach, etc.).

Abbreviations

t = teaspoon   T = Tablespoon   c = cup
oz = ounce   # = pound   qt = quart

Abridged Glossary of Terms

To make good soup, the pot must only simmer or smile.
—A French Proverb

Char Blacken the surface of vegetables by holding them directly in the flame of a gas range or by leaving them on the heating element of an electric stove.

Chop Cut into pieces roughly the size of a pea.

Cube Cut into roughly 1/2" cubes.

Deglaze Pour liquid over brown and caramelized pan drippings from sautéed or roasted vegetables; stir and scrape to loosen them from the pan. This liquid is flavorful and rich—great for the soup pot.

Dice Cut into roughly 1/4" pieces.

Garnish Fresh ingredients added to each individual bowl of soup. Garnish suggestions are listed for every soup, and we think they add essential flavor, color and texture.

Mince Cut into tiny pieces the size of a sesame seed.

Purée Liquefy ingredients in a blender or food processor.

Roast Cook in hot oven or under broiler. This brings out sweet, distinctive flavors in many vegetables. (To roast garlic and peppers, see instructions in the section, "Some Basics.")

Sauté Heat oil in heavy pan over medium or medium-high heat. Toss in vegetables and stir to keep them from burning. Always add onions *before* garlic (the small, sticky bits of minced garlic are likely to burn if you put

Sear — them in first.) "Sauté" literally means "to jump" in French.

Sear — Heat a heavy pan coated with a trace amount of oil over high heat. Add vegetables to hot pan in a single layer. When they begin to release their juices, stir gently. This seals in the juices and gives the vegetables a rich flavor. When the pan is nearly dry, scrape the vegetables into a bowl and de-glaze the pan while it's still hot.

Simmer — Essential to the making of soup is simmering. While simmering, the soup temperature remains constant, gently and slowly cooking the soup in order to extract all of the flavors from the ingredients. Don't increase the heat to "hurry up" the process—and never let your soup boil violently away.

Stock — Given the quantity of soup we cook at Regent, as well as storage and time limitations, we did not make stock from scratch. In previous years, the soups relied on bouillon to make a flavorful broth. Wanting to avoid this packaged, processed, extremely salty (and often full of MSG) substitute, we chose soups that did not require a stock, but relied on the cooking liquid from beans and legumes or other strongly flavored bases (such as tomatoes, coconut milk or peanut butter) that produce rich, flavorful soups. We also experimented with various seasonings and aromatics to enhance the flavor of the soup. We have listed our favorite "flavor boosters" here. That said, good soup is only made better by using a good, homemade stock—and good stock is essential for more subtle and delicate broths.

Toast — Toasting many dried spices and herbs draws out their essential oils and makes them even more aromatic and flavorful. Toast dried herbs (such as leaf oregano) or spices (such as cumin seed or coriander seed) in a toaster oven on light–medium. Or, toast them in a dry, heavy skillet over low heat, shaking the pan often to keep them from burning, until they release their aroma, about 1–2 minutes. Grind toasted seeds with a mortar and pestle. *Note:* Only toast as much as you need for a particular recipe, since toasted spices do not store well.

Some Basics

Favorite Flavor Boosters
- Roasted garlic
- Roasted red pepper purée
- Chutney or Pickapeppa sauce (a concentrated Jamaican specialty sauce made with tomatoes, onions, vinegar, mangoes, raisins & tamarind)
- Splashes of tamari or soy sauce
- Hot sauce or curry paste
- Bundles of fresh herbs added to the soup while simmering, then removed before serving
- Charred onions, garlic or ginger simmered in the soup pot, then removed before serving
- Splashes of sherry, red or white wine added to sauté
- Splashes of red wine vinegar or balsamic vinegar
- The juice of a freshly squeezed lime, lemon or orange added near the end of the cooking time

To Roast Garlic

Rub whole heads of garlic (skins on) with a bit of olive oil, salt and pepper. Roast (uncovered or covered) at about 350°F until you can smell the rich aroma (around 30 minutes). The skins will begin to brown and you will be able to pierce the cloves with a knife. Allow the head to cool, cut the stem end off with a serrated knife, and squeeze the roasted garlic directly into the soup pot.

To Roast Sweet & Mild Peppers

If you're only roasting a few peppers, you can roast it directly in the flame of a gas range (using tongs)—or you can char it on the element of an electric stove. For more peppers, it's easier to roast them in the oven.

Under the broiler or in a 450°F oven, roast the peppers (with stems on) in a pan until they begin to blacken. Turn and continue to roast until all sides are lightly charred. (Don't roast until they're completely black and crispy.) If desired, transfer the peppers into a paper bag or a bowl covered with a tea towel and let the peppers steam. (Some purists deride this because it "overcooks" the peppers.) When they're cool enough to handle, peel off the skins and remove the stems and seeds. (Don't be tempted to wash them beneath running water—you'll wash a good bit of the delicious flavor down the drain.) Be sure to add the sweet juices that have collected in the roasting pan to the soup pot.

Roasted red, yellow or orange pepper strips are lovely sliced up and added to soup toward the end of the cooking time. Or purée the peppers (seeds & stems removed) in a blender or food processor and add directly to the soup.

You can also use the purée as a garnish. Fill a squeeze bottle with the purée (use the roasting juices, a splash of balsamic or red wine vinegar and some olive oil to thin, if desired) and squeeze a colorful ribbon into each bowl of soup.

For a southwestern soup, use dark green poblano or lighter green Anaheim chilies.

To Roast Hot Chili Peppers

To roast hot jalapeños, serranos and other hot chilies, roast them in a dry skillet over high heat until their skins blister. They don't need to be peeled. Remove seeds, or keep some for more heat. Mince the peppers or purée them in a blender with a splash of vinegar, lemon or lime juice. Add the purée (a little at a time) to the soup pot.

To add a smoky heat, toast dried chili peppers in the toaster oven or on a hot dry skillet. (Chipotles, which are smoked jalapeños, and anchos, which are dried poblanos, are two of the best.) Remove the peppers as soon as they puff up like a balloon. Soak toasted chilies in hot water until soft. Remove the stems. Purée the peppers with soaking liquid in a blender. Add the purée to the soup pot (use chipotle purée sparingly; ancho can be used abundantly).

To make your own chili powder, remove the stem of a dried, toasted chili and, leaving in seeds to taste, grind the dried pepper in a mortar and pestle or a blender.

You can also use canned chipotles packed in adobo sauce—a fiery hot purée of smoked jalapeños and vinegar. Purée a whole can and store in the refrigerator or freeze in ice cube trays to keep indefinitely. A little goes a long way.

If the Soup's Too Spicy!

If the soup is too spicy, you can add salt, cooked rice, or potatoes to mellow the heat. Yogurt, sour cream, and cheese—as well as cilantro and grated raw cucumber—are cooling garnishes

Beautiful soup, so rich and green.
Waiting in a hot tureen!
Who for such dainties would not stoop?
Soup of the evening, beautiful soup!
—Lewis Carroll,
Alice in Wonderland

*Ubi caritas
et amor,
ubi caritas,
Deus ibi est.*

–Taizé

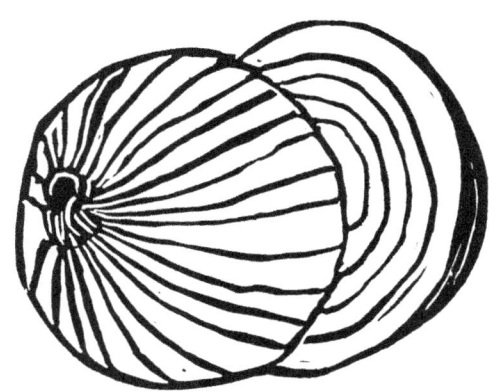

beans

Brazilian Black Bean
serves 6–8

1 # dried black beans
8 c water
2 bay leaves
fresh oregano sprigs (if available)
1 dried ancho or New Mexican
chili pepper OR 1 fresh
 whole jalapeño
2 T olive oil
2 yellow onions (peeled & chopped)
2 t ground cumin
1 t dried leaf oregano
6–8 cloves garlic (peeled & minced)
1/4 c sherry
1 green bell pepper (seeds &
stem removed & diced)
1–2 jalapeño or serrano peppers
(remove seeds/membranes
 and mince OR mince with some
seeds for more heat)
1 15-oz can diced tomatoes, with
juice + 1 t honey OR
 garnish soup with fresh, chopped tomatoes
Juice of 1 orange (about 1/2 c)
salt & pepper to taste

Garnish with sliced green onions, fresh cilantro sprigs, plain yogurt or sour cream and grated Monterey jack or white cheddar cheese.

Rinse and then soak beans over night in plenty of water. OR, for faster method, cover beans with fresh, cold water by 2" and bring to boil. Reduce heat and simmer for 2 minutes. Turn off heat and cover for 2 hours. Drain and rinse well.

Put pre-soaked beans in soup pot with 8 c of fresh, cold water. Add bay leaves, fresh oregano sprigs, dried (or fresh) chili pepper and the orange halves. (Squeeze the orange and set the juice aside to be added toward the end of the cooking time.) Bring to boil. Reduce heat and simmer until beans are tender, about an hour. Remove herbs, orange halves and chili pepper.

Add the diced bell pepper and minced hot pepper to the soup pot as you finish chopping them.

While beans are cooking, heat olive oil over medium heat in heavy pan. Add onion, 1/2 t salt and cumin. Sauté until onion is soft and translucent. Add garlic and oregano and continue to sauté. After a couple minutes, add sherry (optional) and simmer. Once the sherry has been absorbed, add the tomatoes, honey and 1/4 t salt. Continue to simmer for a few minutes.

Once the beans are tender, mash some of the beans against the side of the pot. (For a thicker soup, remove a cup or two of the beans and purée them in a blender or food processor with a bit of the broth, then return the purée to the soup pot.) When the beans are completely tender, add the sautéed vegetables and some freshly ground black pepper. (If the beans aren't tender, the salt in the sauté will make the beans tough.)

Add orange juice towards the end of the cooking

time and let simmer another 5 minutes or so to allow the flavors to blend.

Taste and adjust seasonings. Add honey if the tomatoes are still too acidic (an unmistakable metallic taste that comes from the can). Add additional water if the consistency seems too thick.

Variations

For a *Cuban black bean soup,* increase the olive oil to 1/4 c; add 1 t thyme to the sauté; omit the orange juice; replace the sherry with 2 T red wine vinegar; serve over cooked white rice; garnish with chopped white onion.

For *black bean chili,* decrease water to 6 c; add 1 t ground coriander and 1 T good-quality chili powder to the sauté and increase the cumin to 2 t; add 1 red bell pepper (seeds & stem removed & diced), 2 carrots (scrubbed & diced) and 2 stalks celery (diced) directly to the soup pot; use a 28-oz (rather than 15-oz) can of tomatoes.

For a *New Mexican style soup,* use the juice of 1 lime in place of the oranges (add juice just before serving to sharpen the flavors; don't simmer beans with the lime halves). *Garnish* with avocado slices, crumbled feta cheese, and minced fresh oregano.

Cooking dinner without onions is like playing Scrabble with only consonants on your tray.

—Crescent Dragonwagon,
Soup & Bread: A Country Inn Cookbook

Louisiana Red Beans with Rice
serves 6–8

1 # dried red beans
8 c water
2 bay leaves
fresh sage &/or oregano sprigs (if available)
1 dried chili pepper OR 1 fresh whole jalapeño
2 T olive oil
2 yellow onions (peeled & chopped)
6–8 cloves garlic (peeled & minced)
1/8 t ground allspice
1/8 t ground cloves
1/2 t cinnamon
1 T soy sauce
2 t ancho chili powder (or other good-quality chili powder)
1/2 t chipotle chili powder OR chipotle chili purée (or
 1/4 t ground cayenne)
1 green bell pepper (seeds & stem removed & diced)
1 red pepper (seeds & stem removed & diced)
1–2 jalapeño or serrano peppers (remove seeds/membranes
 and mince OR mince with some seeds for more heat)
2 ribs celery (diced)
2 carrots (scrubbed & diced)
salt & pepper to taste

Serve over white rice. *Garnish* with hot sauce and sliced green onions.

Rinse, then soak beans over night in plenty of water. OR, for faster method, cover beans with fresh, cold water by 2" and bring to boil. Reduce heat and simmer for 2 minutes. Turn off heat and cover for 2 hours. Drain beans and rinse well.

Put pre-soaked beans in soup pot with 8 c of fresh, cold water. Add bay leaves, fresh herb sprigs and chili pepper. Bring to boil. Reduce heat and simmer until beans are tender, about an hour. Remove herbs and chili pepper.

Add the diced carrots and bell peppers, minced hot peppers, and diced celery to the soup pot as you finish chopping each vegetable (in that order).

While beans are cooking, heat olive oil over medium heat in heavy pan. Add onion, 1/2 t salt, allspice and cloves. Sauté until onion is soft and translucent. Add garlic and cinnamon and continue to sauté. Then stir in chili powders. (You may need to add a splash of water or red wine vinegar to keep sauté from sticking.)

When the beans are completely tender, add the sautéed vegetables and soy sauce. (If the beans aren't tender, the salt will make the beans tough.) Continue to simmer until the beans have broken down, stirring often to prevent the beans from sticking and burning (which will add an unpleasant smoky flavor to your soup).

Add some freshly ground pepper and simmer for 5 minutes or so to allow the flavors to blend. Taste and adjust seasonings.

Tuscan White Bean
serves 6–8

1 # dried white beans (any small variety)
8 c water
fresh rosemary sprigs
2 fresh sage leaves
2 bay leaves
2 T olive oil
1 yellow onion (peeled & chopped)
6–8 cloves garlic (peeled & minced)
1 t dried leaf basil
1 t dried leaf oregano
1/2 t dried thyme
1/4 c dry white wine
1 15-oz can diced tomatoes (with juice) + 1 t honey OR
1 # fresh tomatoes (peeled & seeded, roughly chopped)
salt & pepper to taste

Garnish with freshly grated Parmesan cheese and minced fresh rosemary or chopped fresh Italian parsley. A swirl of roasted red pepper purée makes a lovely garnish as well.

Rinse, then soak beans over night in plenty of water. OR, for faster method, cover beans with fresh, cold water by 2" and bring to boil. Reduce heat and simmer for 2 minutes. Turn off heat and cover for 2 hours.

Drain beans and rinse well.

Put pre-soaked beans in soup pot with 8 c of fresh, cold water. Add bay leaf, fresh sage leaves and rosemary sprigs. Bring to boil. Reduce heat and simmer for an hour or so, until beans are tender, about an hour. Remove bay leaves and herbs.

While beans are cooking, heat olive oil over medium heat in heavy pan. Add onion and 1/2 t salt. Sauté until onion is soft and translucent. Add garlic and basil and continue to sauté. After a couple minutes, add white wine and simmer. Once the wine has been absorbed, add the tomatoes, honey and 1/4 t salt and simmer for a few minutes. (If using fresh tomatoes, you don't need to simmer them with the honey in the sauté mixture; just stir the tomatoes directly into soup pot after the sauté.)

Once the beans are tender, add the sauté mixture to the pot. (If the beans aren't tender, the salt in the sauté will make the beans tough.) Continue to simmer until the beans have broken down, stirring often to prevent the beans from sticking and burning (which will add an unpleasant smoky flavor to your soup). Add some freshly ground pepper and simmer the soup for a few minutes to allow the flavors to blend.

Taste and adjust seasonings. Add honey if the tomatoes are still too acidic (an unmistakable metallic taste that comes from the can). Add additional water if the consistency seems too thick.

Variations

For added color, stir in 1 bunch of spinach (washed, stems removed, sliced into thin ribbons) about 5–10 minutes before serving.

Or replace the canned tomatoes (and omit the honey) with 8–12 sun-dried tomatoes (sliced thin). Add them to the sauté before adding the wine.

Add 1/2 c sliced green (pitted) olives to the soup pot in the last 5–10 minutes of cooking time.

For a richer soup with a smoky aroma, roast 1 head of garlic and mash roasted cloves with some additional olive, salt and pepper. (See *Some Basics* for instructions.) Add this paste to the soup pot when you add the sauté.

For *Portuguese kale minestra*, omit the canned tomatoes and honey. Add an additional 2 c of water. Replace the fresh rosemary with fresh thyme. Add 1 # Yukon gold or russet potatoes (scrubbed & cubed) to the soup pot roughly 45 minutes into the cooking of the beans. Continue to simmer soup until the beans and potatoes break down. Instead of spinach, add 1 bunch of kale (washed, trimmed and sliced into thin ribbons) to the soup about 10 minutes after adding the potatoes.

Soup as a main course, soup to begin the meal—and when it is homemade, it is soup to nourish the soul.
—Julia Child,
The French Chef Cookbook

*Praise God from whom all blessings flow.
Praise God all creatures here below.
Praise God above all heavenly host.
Praise Father, Son and Holy Ghost. Amen.*

—Bishop Thomas Ken

(first published in 1709)

legumes

Arkansas Black-Eyed Pea
serves 6–8

1 # dried black-eyed peas
8 c water
2 bay leaves
1 dried chili pepper OR 1 fresh whole jalapeño
2 T olive oil
2 yellow onions (peeled & chopped)
6–8 cloves garlic (peeled & minced)
1 T ground cumin
1 t ground coriander
1/2 t dried leaf oregano
1/2 t dried leaf basil
1/2 t dried thyme
2 carrots (scrubbed & diced)
2 celery stalks (diced)
1 green bell pepper (seeds & stem removed & diced)
1 red bell pepper (seeds & stem removed & diced)
1–2 jalapeño or serrano peppers (remove seeds/membranes and mince OR mince with some seeds for more heat)
1 16-oz can crushed tomatoes (or tomato purée) + 2 t honey
1 T soy sauce or tamari
1 T Pickapeppa (optional)
salt & pepper to taste

Garnish with fresh cilantro sprigs, sliced green onions, diced fresh tomatoes, grated smoked cheese and hot sauce.

Rinse black-eyed peas well. Place in pot with 8 c fresh, cold water, bay leaf, fresh herbs and dried (or fresh) chili pepper. Bring to boil. Reduce heat and simmer.

After roughly 20 minutes, add carrots and green pepper. Continue to simmer until black-eyed peas are tender, about 30 minutes. Remove bay leaf, fresh herbs and chili pepper. Add crushed tomatoes, honey, soy sauce and Pickapeppa.

While black-eyed peas are cooking, sauté onion in olive oil over medium heat. Add 1/2 t salt, cumin and coriander and sauté until onion is soft and translucent. Add garlic, basil and oregano and continue to sauté. After a couple minutes, add celery, chilies and thyme. (You may need to add a splash of water or red wine vinegar to keep sauté from sticking.)

After a few minutes, or when the pan seems dry, add crushed tomatoes, honey and 1/4 t salt and simmer for a few more minutes.

Once the black-eyed peas are tender, add the tomato-mixture to the pot. (If the black-eyed peas aren't tender, the salt in the sauté will make the beans tough.) Add soy sauce and (optional) Pickapeppa.

Add some freshly ground pepper and simmer for a few minutes to allow the flavors to blend.

Taste and adjust seasonings. Add honey if the tomatoes are still too acidic (an unmistakable metallic taste that comes from the can).

Moroccan Harira
serves 6–8

1 c dried chickpeas
6–8 c water
2 bay leaves
1 c lentils (optional)
2 T olive oil
1 yellow onion (peeled & chopped)
4–6 cloves garlic (peeled & minced)
1 T fresh ginger (peeled & grated)
1 carrot (scrubbed & diced)
2 stalks celery (diced)
1 15-oz can whole tomatoes, puréed with juice + 1 t honey
 OR 1 # fresh plum tomatoes, puréed
1 t ground cumin
1/2 t ground paprika
1/2 t ground cinnamon
1/4 t ground allspice
1/4 t ground cayenne (more if desired)
1/2 t turmeric
small pinch of saffron threads (optional)
Juice of 1 lemon
salt & pepper to taste

Garnish with fresh sprigs of cilantro or chopped fresh mint.

Rinse, then soak chickpeas over night in plenty of water. OR, for faster method, cover chickpeas with fresh, cold water by 2" and bring to boil. Reduce heat and simmer for 2 minutes. Turn off heat and cover for 2 hours.

Drain chickpeas and rinse well.

Put pre-soaked chickpeas in soup pot with 6 c of fresh, cold water (8 c if using lentils). Add bay leaves and bring to boil. Reduce heat and simmer until chickpeas begin to soften, about an hour. Rinse and add (optional) lentils and continue to simmer until the lentils and chickpeas are tender, about 30–45 minutes. Remove bay leaves.

While the chickpeas are cooking, heat olive oil over medium heat. Add onion, 1/2 t salt and cumin. Sauté until onion is soft and translucent. Add garlic, fresh ginger and paprika. After a couple minutes, add carrot, cinnamon and allspice. After a few minutes, add celery, cayenne and turmeric. (You may need to add a splash or two of water to keep the sauté from sticking.)

When vegetables are tender, stir the puréed tomatoes into the sauté, along with the honey and 1/4 t salt. Add (optional) saffron and some freshly ground pepper. Continue to simmer for a few minutes.

Once the chickpeas (and lentils) are tender, stir in the tomato mixture, lemon juice and fresh parsley. (If the chickpeas aren't tender, the salt in the sauté will make them tough.) Add some freshly ground pepper and simmer for about 10 minutes to allow the flavors to blend.

Taste and adjust seasonings. Add honey if the tomatoes are still too acidic (an unmistakable metallic taste that comes from the can).

If desired, thicken soup by dissolving 2 T flour in 1/4 c cold water to make a paste. Whisk a ladle full of the hot soup broth into the paste until thoroughly mixed. Then pour the mixture back into the soup pot. Stir continuously so that the soup thickens without lumps.

*Small cheer and great welcome
make a merry feast.*
—William Shakespeare

Spicy Mexican Lentil with Roasted Chilies & Garlic
serves 6

1 c lentils
6 c fresh water
1 bay leaf
2 fresh sage leaves
1 fresh oregano and/or marjoram sprig
1 head garlic (whole, unpeeled)
2 T olive oil
1 15-oz can whole tomatoes (with juice) + 1 t honey OR
 1 # whole tomatoes (peeled & seeded)
1 yellow onion (peeled & chopped)
1 t ground cumin
1/2 t chipotle chili powder OR
chipotle chili purée OR
1/4 t ground cayenne
1/2 t dried leaf oregano
1 carrot (scrubbed & diced)
2 stalks celery (diced)
1 red bell pepper (seeds & stem removed & diced)
2–3 Anaheim, poblano or other
mild fresh chilies, roasted
 & chopped (see *Some Basics* for instructions) OR
1 5-oz can roasted mild green chilies, chopped

Garnish with fresh cilantro sprigs and/or chopped fresh oregano, sour cream or yogurt, and grated Monterey jack cheese.

Rinse the lentils well, then place them in a soup pot with 6 of fresh, cold water. Add bay leaf and fresh herbs. Bring to boil, then reduce the heat and simmer, until the lentils are tender, about 30 minutes. Remove the bay leaf and herbs.

While the lentils are cooking, preheat the oven to 350ºF. Rub the head of garlic with olive oil and sprinkle with salt and pepper. Place it on a baking sheet and roast for about 30 minutes, until soft. When the garlic has cooled, slice off the stem end and squeeze the garlic out of its skin. Purée the garlic with the tomatoes in a blender or food processor and set aside.

While the garlic is roasting, heat olive oil over medium heat in a large, heavy pan. Add onion, 1/2 t salt and cumin. Sauté until onion is soft and translucent. Add carrot, celery, bell pepper and oregano and sauté for a few more minutes. Add the tomato purée, roasted green chilies, chipotle chili powder (or chipotle chili purée or ground cayenne) and another 1/4 t salt and simmer for about 10 minutes.

When the lentils are tender, add the tomato mixture to the soup pot. (If the lentils aren't tender, the salt in the sauté will make them tough.) Add some freshly ground pepper and simmer for several minutes to allow the flavors to blend.

Taste and adjust seasonings. Add honey if the tomatoes are still too acidic (an unmistakable metallic taste that comes from the can).

This soup is even better the next day.

Variations

For the following variations, omit all the fresh herbs, dried herbs and spices, roasted garlic and roasted chilies from the preceding recipe and make the noted adjustments.

For *Moroccan lentil,* omit above as noted; add 1 t ground cumin to the sauté with the onions; add 6 garlic cloves (peeled & minced) and 1 T fresh ginger (peeled & grated) to the sauté after the onions are soft, along with 1/2 t ground coriander, 1/2 t turmeric and 1/4 t ground cayenne. Replace the tomato purée with either fresh or canned chopped tomatoes OR, instead of tomatoes, add the juice of 1–2 lemons, along with the grated zest from 1 lemon. This soup is also good with spinach added towards the end of the cooking time (see *Turkish lentil* variation below for directions). *Garnish* with fresh cilantro sprigs and plain yogurt.

For *Turkish lentil,* omit above as noted; add some fresh sprigs of rosemary with the bay leaf (and remove with the bay leaf after the lentils are tender); add 4 garlic cloves (peeled & minced) to the sauté after the onions are soft, along with 1/2 t dried leaf oregano. Replace the tomato purée with either fresh or canned chopped tomatoes. Stir in 1 bunch of Swiss chard leaves or spinach (washed, stemmed and sliced into 1/2" ribbons) in the last 5 minutes (spinach) or 10 minutes (chard) of the cooking time. *Garnish* with chopped fresh parsley, minced fresh rosemary or chopped fresh mint and lemon wedges. To make this version spicy, add 1/4 t cayenne to the sauté.

Surely one of the greatest satisfactions of life is to cook a really delicious meal, a meal that nourishes the body and cheers the spirit, and may be remembered with pleasure for a long time to come.
—Rose Elliot,
The Festive Vegetarian

Swedish Split Pea
serves 6

    2 c dried yellow split peas
    8 c water
    1 bay leaf
    a few fresh marjoram (or oregano) and/or thyme sprigs (if available)
    1 potato (cubed)
    2 carrots (diced)
    2 ribs celery (diced)
    1 T olive oil
    2 yellow onions (peeled & chopped)
    4 cloves garlic (peeled & minced)
    2 t dried leaf marjoram (or dried leaf oregano)
    1/2 t dried thyme

Garnish with oyster crackers or rye bread croutons.

Rinse split peas. Place them in a soup pot with 8 c fresh, cold water, the bay leaf and the fresh herb sprigs. Bring to boil, then reduce heat and simmer.

Add the potato, carrots and celery as you finish chopping them (in that order). Continue to simmer until the split peas are tender, about 30 minutes. Remove bay leaf and fresh herbs.

Meanwhile, heat olive oil over medium heat in a heavy pan. Add onion and 1/2 t salt. Sauté until onion is soft and translucent. Add the garlic, marjoram and thyme and sauté for a couple more minutes.

Once the split peas are tender, add the sauté to the soup pot, along with some freshly ground pepper. (If the split peas aren't tender, the salt in the sauté will make them tough.) Continue to simmer the soup, stirring often to prevent the split peas from sticking to the bottom and burning, until everything is tender, about 30 minutes.

Taste and adjust seasonings.

Variation

To make *split pea with caraway seeds,* use green split peas instead of yellow. Add 1 T caraway seeds and 1 whole fresh jalapeño to the soup pot, along with the bay leaf and fresh herbs. Follow the rest of the directions, but omit dried marjoram and thyme. Add 1 T soy sauce or Pickapeppa.

Thai-Vietnamese Fusion: Peanut *Phô*
serves 6

1 head garlic (unpeeled, whole)
2 yellow onions (unpeeled, whole)
2" piece of ginger (unpeeled)
2 fresh serrano or Thai bird chilies (whole)
2 carrots (scrubbed & cut into 3" pieces)
3 stalks celery (cleaned & cut into 3" pieces)
6 medium dried Chinese black mushrooms, rinsed (optional)
4 whole star anise
4 whole cloves
8–12 whole black peppercorns
1/4 c soy sauce
1/2 c smooth peanut butter (use a natural variety without sugar, salt or hydrogenated oil)
1 t +/− green curry paste (optional, to taste)
1 # dried rice noodles (flat variety, small 1/16"-width size)

Garnishes
2 c mung bean sprouts (washed very well)
1/2 bunch green onions (sliced)
1/2 bunch cilantro (washed & trimmed into small sprigs)
1 bunch Thai basil (washed & trimmed into small sprigs)
1 lime, cut into wedges
2 fresh serrano or Thai bird chilies (cut into thin rings)
1/2 c peanuts (toasted & chopped)

Making phô (pronounced "fuh") is a labor of love, but the nourishing, flavorful broth is well worth the effort.

Char the onions over an open flame or place them directly on a medium-hot electric burner. Turn with tongs until all the edges are slightly blackened. Peel and discard the blackened skins. Cut the ginger in half lengthwise and then bruise with the flat side of a knife. Char it as you did the onions. Rinse the ginger. Char the garlic in the same manner. Remove the charred paper skin. Char the fresh chilies in the same manner.

Bring 4 quarts of water to a boil in a soup pot. Add the charred onions, ginger, garlic and chilies, along with the carrots, celery and (optional) dried mushrooms. Reduce heat and simmer for at least an hour—but preferably two.

While the broth is simmering, toast the whole star anise, cloves and peppercorns in a dry skillet on low to medium-low heat. Stir and shake until the spices release their fragrant aroma and darken slightly, just a minute or two. Transfer to a bowl (they'll continue to cook if you leave them in the pan.)

Place the rice noodles in a pot of cold water and soak them for 30 minutes. Drain and rinse well to remove excess starch (which will make noodles sticky), then set aside. Bring a large pot of water to a rolling boil. Keep the water simmering on low until you're ready to *serve* the *phô*.

When the spices are cool enough to handle, place them in a spice bag or tie in a square of cheesecloth. Add to the broth and simmer for 30 minutes, then remove and discard. (Simmering the spices any longer will make the broth too strong.)

After removing the spices, add the peanut butter, soy sauce and (optional) green curry paste to the broth. Taste and adjust seasonings. The broth should be pungent and spicy. The peanut butter should add a rich complexity, but it shouldn't overpower the other flavors.

While the broth continues to simmer, prepare all the garnishes and put them in attractive serving bowls. (Garnishes are to be added individually, at the table.)

Preheat the soup bowls (*phô* works best served in large, deep bowls) by placing them in a warm oven for several minutes.

Before serving, remove all of the vegetables and mushrooms from the broth with a large slotted spoon. Discard vegetables—all that remains is the flavorful broth.

When you're ready to serve the *phô*, bring the water back to a rolling boil over high heat. Place the noodles in the boiling water. Stir so the noodles untangle and cook evenly. Blanch until soft but still chewy, about 20 seconds. Drain noodles completely.

To serve, divide the noodles among 4 large (or 6 medium) preheated bowls. (If the noodles are no longer hot, briefly dip them in hot water.) Pour a generous amount of hot broth over the noodles. Invite guests to garnish their own bowls, noting that the success of this soup is completely dependent upon the fresh garnishes.

Serve *phô* with chopsticks (or forks) and spoons.

Optional Additions

Cut 8 oz of tofu into 1/4"-thick slices. Pan-sear in 2 T of oil over medium heat in a heavy pan. Cook until golden, turning once, about 5 minutes. Top noodles with tofu before adding broth.

Blanch broccoli florets or carrot coins (carrots sliced thinly on the diagonal), separately, in plenty of boiling water until bright green or orange. Scoop out with a slotted spoon, drain, then plunge in cold water to stop the cooking process. Top noodles with blanched vegetables before adding broth. (You can also use a variety of other vegetables, such as bok choy, cauliflower, celery or seared mushrooms. Just pre-cook the vegetables enough so that they are crisp-tender when you pour the hot broth over them. (Don't cook the vegetables in the broth itself.)

Add 1 small head Savoy or Napa cabbage (cored & sliced into thin 2–3" long ribbons) to the soup pot after removing all the vegetables and dried mushrooms from the broth.

Spicy West African Peanut
serves 6

4 c stock or water
1 bay leaf
2 sweet potatoes (peeled & cut into 1" chunks)
1 beet (peeled & cut into 1" chunks)
2 carrots (scrubbed & cut into 1" chunks)
2 T olive oil
2 yellow onions (peeled & chopped)
6 cloves garlic (peeled & minced)
2 t fresh ginger (peeled & grated)
1/2 t cayenne
1 c smooth peanut butter (use a natural variety without sugar, salt or hydrogenated oil)
1 16-oz can whole tomatoes with juice

Garnish with sliced green onions or chives.

Note: For a less sweet soup, you can substitute 1 russet potato for 1 of the sweet potatoes.

Place the stock or water in a soup pot with the bay leaf. Add the sweet potato, potato, beet and carrots. Bring to a boil, then reduce heat and simmer, uncovered, until the vegetables are tender, about 15–20 minutes.

Meanwhile, heat the olive oil over medium heat in a heavy pan. Add onion and 1/2 t salt. Sauté until onion is soft and translucent. Stir in the garlic, ginger and cayenne and sauté for a couple more minutes. Add to soup pot, deglazing pan with a splash of stock or water.

When all the vegetables in the soup pot are tender, purée them, with the tomatoes, in a blender or food processor. (You may have to do this in batches.) Return the purée to the soup pot. Stir in the peanut butter until soup is uniform and smooth.

Taste and adjust seasonings. The sweetness of the soup will depend upon the carrots, sweet potato and beet. If you think it needs to be sweeter, add a teaspoon or so of honey to enhance the natural sugars in the vegetables.

Reheat soup on low, stirring often to prevent it from sticking and scorching. Add more water, stock or tomato purée to thin soup, if desired.

*O, the Lord is good to me,
and so I thank the Lord,
for giving me the things I need—
the sun and the rain and the apple seed.
The Lord is good to me.
Amen.*

–anonymous

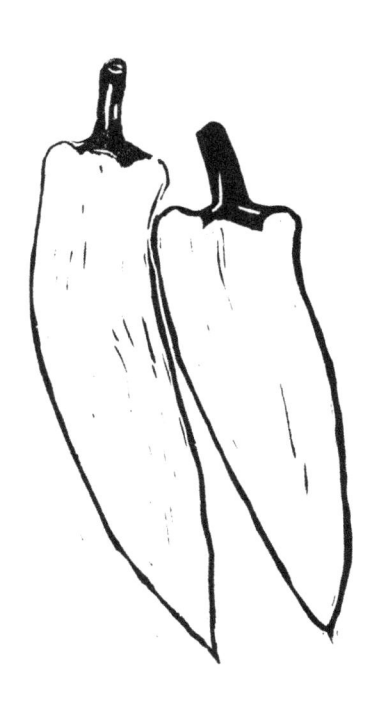

chilies

New Mexican Chili Potato
serves 6–8

4 large tomatoes, halved lengthwise
8 c water or stock
2 large potatoes (cut into 1/2" cubes)
1 red bell pepper
1 yellow bellow pepper
6 medium poblano chilies
6 medium Anaheim chilies
1 jalapeño chili
2 serrano chilies
juice of 1 lime
1/2 t chipotle chili purée (optional)
2 T olive oil
2 yellow onions (peeled & chopped)
6–8 cloves garlic (peeled & minced)
1/2 t ground cumin

Garnish with fresh cilantro sprigs, grated smoked cheese or crumbled *queso fresco* (fresh Mexican specialty cheese similar to feta) and lime wedges.

Preheat the broiler. Arrange the tomato halves (cut sides down) on a baking sheet. Drizzle with a bit of olive oil and sprinkle with salt and pepper. Broil until the skins are charred. Run the broiled tomatoes through a food mill to (if you want to remove the seeds and skins) OR purée them in a food processor. Transfer the purée to a large soup pot. Add the fresh, cold water or stock and the potatoes and bring to a boil. Reduce heat and simmer until the potatoes are tender, about 20 minutes.

Meanwhile, roast the bell peppers and the poblano and Anaheim chilies. (See *Some Basics* for directions on roasting peppers.) Peel the peppers and chilies and discard the stems and seeds. Cut the chilies into short 1/4"-wide strips. Set the roasted bell peppers aside.

Sear the whole jalapeños and serranos in a dry skillet over high heat until they are charred. Remove stems and the seeds. (For a spicier soup, leave in some of the seeds.) Purée the roasted hot chilies and bell peppers in a blender or food processor with 1/4 t salt, the lime juice and the (optional) chipotle chili purée. Stir the purée into the soup pot.

Heat olive oil over medium heat in a heavy pan. Add onion and 1/2 t salt. Sauté until onion is soft and translucent. Add the garlic and cumin and continue to sauté for a few minutes. (You may need to add a splash of water to keep the sauté from sticking.)

Transfer the sauté to the soup pot and continue to simmer for another 5 minutes.

Taste and adjust seasonings.

Jubilate Deo!
Jubilate Deo!
Alleluia!
– Michael Praetorius
(c. sixteenth century)

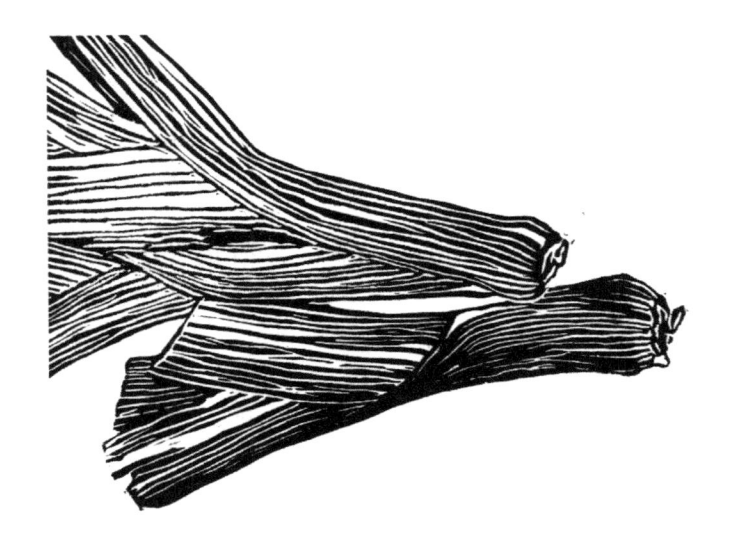

leeks

Potato Leek
serves 6–8

6 c stock or water
bay leaf
2 # russet, Yukon Gold or Yellow Finn potatoes (scrubbed & sliced thin)
2 T olive oil (a bit more if omitting butter)
2 T butter (optional)
6 leeks (white and tender green parts only; cut in half lengthwise; washed well; sliced crosswise)
8 cloves garlic (peeled & minced)
1/4 c dry white wine
salt & pepper to taste

Garnish with Parmesan cheese, sliced green onions or chopped fresh parsley, and plain yogurt or sour cream.

Well did he love garlic, onions, and eke leeks, and for to drinken strong wine, red as blood.
—Geoffrey Chaucer,
Canterbury Tales

Place the potatoes and water or stock in a soup pot, along with bay leaf, 1/2 t salt and a few pinches of pepper. Bring to a boil, then reduce heat and simmer, uncovered, until the potatoes begin to break down, about 30 minutes.

While the potatoes are cooking, heat the olive oil and (optional) butter over medium heat in a heavy pan. Add the leeks, 1/2 t salt and some pepper. Sauté until the leeks begin to soften. Add garlic and sauté for another few minutes. Then add wine and simmer, uncovered, until the pan is nearly dry.

Remove the bay leaf from the soup pot and mash the potatoes against the side of the pot. Add the sauté, along with more stock or water to thin soup (if desired).

Cover and cook over low heat for 20–30 minutes. Taste and adjust seasonings.

Variations

For a distinctive flavor, add 1 fennel bulb (trimmed & diced) to the sauté along with the garlic and sauté until soft. Use the feathery fennel tops (minced) as an additional garnish.

Instead of adding fresh garlic to the sauté, add a whole head of roasted, mashed garlic to the soup pot along with the sautéed leeks.

Replace half the leeks with 2 yellow onions (peeled & thinly sliced), then caramelized over low heat for 30–45 minutes before adding to the soup pot).

Garnish with a swirl of roasted red pepper purée.

*For life and health and daily food,
we give Thee thanks, O Lord. Amen.*
　　　　　–anonymous (traditional)

potatoes

Monastic Cheese & Potato
serves 6–8

1 16-oz good quality pale ale or dark beer
2 # russet potatoes (scrubbed & sliced 1/4" thick)
4 c water or stock
2 bay leaves
1 T butter
2 T olive oil
1 yellow onion (peeled & chopped)
8 cloves garlic (peeled & minced)
1/2 t dried leaf basil
1/2 t dried leaf oregano
1 rib celery (diced)
1 carrot (scrubbed & diced)
1 15-oz can whole tomatoes (with juice) + 1 t honey OR
1 # fresh tomatoes, roughly chopped
1 T soy sauce or tamari
2 t Pickapeppa (optional)
Several dashes hot sauce (or 1/4 t cayenne)
1–2 t dry mustard
2 T all-purpose flour
1/2 c heavy cream (can add more for a richer soup, if desired)
8 oz extra-sharp white or yellow grated cheddar cheese (can add more for a richer soup, if desired)

Garnish with finely chopped fresh parsley or green onions.

Pour the beer into a heavy soup pot. Add the potatoes and enough fresh, cold water or stock to cover. Add the bay leaves. Bring to a boil, then turn down the heat and let simmer, covered, until the potatoes are tender, about 30 minutes. Add remaining water.

Meanwhile, heat the butter and olive oil over medium heat in a heavy pan. Add onion and 1/2 t salt. Sauté until onion is soft and translucent. Add the garlic, basil and oregano and continue to sauté for a few minutes. Add the celery and carrot and sauté for a couple minutes more. Stir in the chopped tomatoes, soy sauce and (optional) Pickapeppa. Increase the heat to medium-high and simmer, stirring constantly, until the liquid evaporates and the mixture becomes a thick paste, about 15 minutes. Slowly sprinkle the flour over the mixture while stirring, cooking the mixture for another couple minutes. Then add the hot pepper sauce and dry mustard.

Transfer the mixture to the soup pot and turn down the heat so that it barely simmers.

To add the cream to the soup without curdling it, pull a cupful of hot soup out of the soup pot. Whisk the soup broth into the measured cream. Slowly add the soup/cream mixture back to the soup pot, stirring constantly. Do not let the soup return to a boil after this point, or the milk will curdle. (It's still fine to eat—it just won't look as nice.)

With the soup barely simmering, slowly stir in the grated cheddar cheese and some freshly ground pepper. Continue to cook, stirring constantly, until the cheese is melted and the potatoes have broken down, about 20 minutes. Keep the heat very low and stir often (to keep the soup from sticking and scorching) until you're ready to serve the soup.

Taste and adjust seasonings.

This soup tastes wonderful reheated, though you may need to add a little stock or milk to thin it.

Of soup and love, the first is best.
—Spanish Proverb

*Come take this bread,
come share this cup,
the presence of the Lord is near.*

–"Gather Around," Unless the Seed Falls

corn

Summer Corn, Zucchini & Chili Chowder
serves 6–8

6–8 c water or stock
1 bay leaf
2–3 fresh oregano sprigs (if available)
1 dried ancho chili pepper OR
1 fresh whole jalapeño
3–4 potatoes (scrubbed & diced)
2 carrots (scrubbed & diced)
2 celery stalks (diced)
1 red bell pepper (seeds & stem removed; diced)
1 zucchini (unpeeled; cut in half lengthwise & sliced)
1 T olive oil
1 T butter
1 yellow onion (peeled & chopped)
6 cloves garlic (peeled & minced)
2 t ground cumin
1 t dried leaf oregano
1/4–1/2 t chipotle chili powder
1–2 jalapeño or serrano peppers (remove seeds/membranes and mince OR mince with some seeds for more heat)
1 (optional) medium leek (white and tender green parts only; cut in half lengthwise; washed well; sliced crosswise)
2 T all-purpose flour
2 c milk (any variety but skim)
3–4 c whole-kernel corn cut fresh off the cob
salt & pepper to taste

Garnish with sour cream or plain yogurt, fresh cilantro sprigs, chopped fresh tomatoes and (optional) crumbled *queso fresco* or grated pepper jack cheese.

Put stock or water in pot over medium-high heat with bay leaf, fresh oregano sprigs and dried (or fresh) chili pepper.

As you finish chopping each vegetable, add it to the stock. (Add potato first, then carrots, celery, red pepper, zucchini and corn.) Simmer vegetables on low until tender, about 20 minutes.

While vegetables are cooking, melt butter with olive oil over medium heat in heavy pan. Add onion, 1/2 t salt and cumin and sauté. When onion is soft, add garlic, oregano and minced chili. Continue to sauté until onion is translucent. Add (optional) leek and (optional) chipotle chili powder and sauté for another couple minutes. (You may need to add a bit of water or stock to the sauté to keep the sauté from sticking.) Turn down the heat to medium-low and stir. Then sprinkle the flour over the sauté and cook another minute, stirring constantly. Gradually add the milk, stirring to smooth any lumps, and cook until thickened, another minute or so. Add sauté to soup pot, deglazing the sauté pan with some stock or water.

Remove the bay leaf and the chili pepper from the soup pot. Pull the stem off the whole chili, then place it (with seeds to taste) in blender or food processor. Add about two cups of vegetables from the soup pot and purée until smooth. Return the purée to the soup pot. Add some freshly ground pepper and simmer for a few more minutes.

Taste and adjust seasonings.

Adjust to desired consistency. Purée additional soup to make it thicker. Or, if the soup seems too thick, thin by adding additional stock or milk.

Variations

For a richer soup, purée 1/2 c cream with the vegetables, then stir purée slowly back into the soup pot.

To make in wintertime, use frozen corn and add 1 16-oz can diced tomatoes (with juice and 1 t honey) to the sauté before adding the flour and milk. Omit the zucchini and red bell pepper.

For an even sweeter flavor, roast 1 medium butternut squash (or other sweet variety), along with several cloves of garlic. (Refer to one of the pumpkin/butternut squash recipes in this book for instructions on roasting and puréeing the squash.) Add this purée to the soup pot with the sauté.

For a simple chowder without the New Mexican flare, omit the zucchini, hot peppers, cumin and oregano. Replace the red bell pepper with a green pepper. *Garnish* with chopped fresh parsley and Hungarian paprika.

Eat soup first and eat it last, and live till a hundred years be past.
—French Proverb

*Rejoice in the Lord always,
and again I say rejoice.
Rejoice! Rejoice! And again I say rejoice!*

–anonymous (adaptation of Phil 4:4–7)

mushrooms

Tomato Mushroom Bisque
8–10 servings

> 10 c water
> 1 28-oz can diced tomatoes + 1 T honey
> 1 5-oz can tomato paste
> 2 T olive oil
> 2 yellow onions (peeled & chopped)
> 6–8 cloves garlic (peeled & minced)
> 4 stalks celery (diced)
> 1 T dried leaf oregano
> 1 T dried basil
> 3/4 # white button mushrooms (sliced)
> 1/4 c heavy cream
> 1/4–1/2 c grated Parmesan cheese
> salt & pepper to taste

Note: You can substitute 1/2 c whole milk for the cream, if desired.

Garnish with additional Parmesan cheese.

Heat diced tomatoes, tomato paste and water in a stockpot over medium-high heat. Add honey and simmer gently.

Heat the olive oil over medium heat in a heavy pan. Add the onion and 1/2 t salt. Sauté until onion is soft and translucent.

Add garlic, basil and oregano and continue to sauté for a few minutes. Add the celery and sauté for a couple more minutes. Scrape the sauté into the soup pot, deglazing the pan with a little of the tomato broth. Continue to simmer until vegetables are tender, about 30 minutes.

Meanwhile, sear mushrooms in 2–3 batches over high heat in a heavy pan coated with just a bit of oil. (Don't crowd the pan or you'll end up boiling the mushrooms.) As the mushrooms brown, they will release their juices. Add a dash of salt and a pinch of pepper to each batch. When the mushrooms release their juices, stir gently. When the pan is nearly dry and the mushrooms are golden, scrape them into a bowl and set aside. Deglaze the pan after searing each batch by pouring a splash of water into the hot skillet, then scraping the delicious juices into the soup pot.

To add the cream (or milk) to the soup without curdling it, pull a cupful of hot soup out of the soup pot. Whisk the hot soup into the measured cream (or milk). Slowly add the soup/cream mixture back to the soup pot, stirring constantly. Do not let the soup return to a boil after this point, or the cream will curdle. (It's still fine to eat—it just won't look as nice.) Slowly stir in Parmesan cheese.

About 5 minutes before serving, stir in the seared mushrooms and plenty of freshly ground pepper.
Taste and adjust seasonings. Add additional cream for a richer soup. Add additional honey if the tomatoes are too acidic (an unmistakable metallic taste that comes from the can).

Déjà vu meal:

Make a large batch and serve the leftovers over pasta or use leftover soup as the sauce for lasagna.

Soup is delicious.
Soup is nutritious.
Soup can light the inner fire.
Soup can be hot or cold,
thick or thin.
Soup is healthy,
light and stimulating—
agreeing with almost everyone.
—Bernard Clayton Jr.,
The Complete Book
of Soups and Stews

Asian Wild Mushroom and Leek
serves 6

1 T olive oil
2 shallots (peeled & minced)
4 cloves garlic (peeled & minced)
1 large leek (white and tender
green part only; cut in half
 lengthwise; washed well; sliced crosswise)
1 T fresh ginger (minced or finely grated)
1 T fresh lemongrass (tender
white bulb only; minced)
1/2 t Madras curry powder (this is a hot variety)
5 c vegetable broth (or water)
1/2 c unsweetened coconut milk
1 t cornstarch or flour, whisked with 1–2 T water
1/4 # white mushrooms (stems
removed, caps thinly sliced)
1/2 # wild mushrooms (chanterelles,
shiitakes, morels) OR
 brown mushrooms (portobellos, creminis)
8–12 dried mushrooms (any variety)
1 T soy sauce or tamari mixed with 2 T water
Juice of 1 lemon

Garnish with chopped fresh chives.

In soup pot, heat olive oil over medium-high heat. Add the shallots and 1/2 t salt, stirring until browned. Reduce heat to medium, add the garlic, leek, ginger, lemongrass and curry powder. Sauté for a few more minutes. Pour in the stock, coconut milk and add the dried mushrooms.

In small bowl, whisk the cornstarch or flour with 1–2 T of water. Stir until smooth. Then whisk the paste into the soup and bring to a boil. Reduce heat and simmer for 30 minutes. Taste and adjust seasonings. Fish out the dried mushrooms and discard.

Meanwhile, sear mushrooms in 2–3 batches over high heat in a heavy pan coated with just a bit of oil. (Don't crowd the pan or you'll end up boiling the mushrooms.) As the mushrooms brown, they will release their juices. Add a pinch of salt and pepper to each batch. Keep stirring so that the mushrooms don't burn and/or stick to the pan. Once they have released their juices, set them aside in a bowl. Deglaze the pan after searing each batch of mushrooms by pouring a splash of watered-down soy sauce into the hot skillet, then scraping the delicious juices into the soup pot.

Just before serving, add the seared mushrooms and lemon juice to the soup pot. Taste and adjust seasonings.

*Be present at our table, Lord.
Be here and everywhere adored.
Abide with us and grant that we
May feast in Paradise with Thee. Amen.*

–music, Genevan Psalter (1551); lyrics, British hymnist John Cennick (1741)

winter squash

Thanksgiving Pumpkin Apple Curry
serves 6

 3 c water or stock
1 medium sweet pie pumpkin (roughly 3–4 # whole) OR
 any sweet winter squash, such as butternut or red kuri
1 head garlic (peel individual cloves and leave whole)
2 T olive oil
1 yellow onion (peeled & chopped)
1 T butter
3 crisp apples (stems & cores removed; unpeeled; diced)
1 T curry powder
1/2 c apple juice
1/4 c Calvados (apple brandy), brandy or dry white wine
1 c heavy cream
salt & pepper to taste

Garnish with plain yogurt.

To make an easy stock for this soup, put all the seeds and strings from the pumpkin, stems and cores from the apples and papery skin from the roasted garlic, along with 1 head of garlic (cloves separated, skins left on), 1 onion (unpeeled & quartered) and 1 carrot (scrubbed & quartered) into a pot with 6 c water and 1 t salt. Bring to a boil, reduce heat and simmer for about an hour. Strain and discard the solids.

To roast pumpkin: preheat the oven to 375ºF. Cut pumpkin or squash in half lengthwise. Remove seeds and strings with a spoon. Rub exposed flesh with some olive oil and sprinkle with salt and pepper. Toss whole garlic cloves with olive oil and place them in the empty pumpkin halves. Place pumpkin halves cut-side down on a lightly oiled roasting pan with sides. Roast until tender (when you can pierce the sides easily with a fork), about 30–40 minutes. Set aside until cool enough to handle. Scoop out flesh and purée, along with roasted cloves of garlic, in blender or food processor.

While pumpkin is roasting, heat olive oil over medium-high heat in heavy pan. Add onion and 1/2 t salt and sauté until soft. Reduce heat to medium-low, add some freshly ground pepper and continue to sauté until the onions caramelize (turn a bit brown), about 20 minutes. Add a splash or two of wine or brandy and scrape to keep the sauté from sticking to the pan. Once the onions have caramelized, add half the remaining brandy or white wine and continue to sauté until the pan is almost dry. Scrape the contents into a blender or food processor.

Melt the butter over medium heat in the same sauté pan. Add the diced apples and sauté another couple minutes, stirring often. Add the curry powder and sauté another couple minutes, adding a splash or two of brandy or wine to prevent sticking. When the apples are soft, add the remaining brandy or white wine and cook until the pan is almost dry. Remove from heat.

Place *half* the apple sauté in the blender or food processor, along with the caramelized onions.

Place stock or water in a soup pot. Add remaining apple sauté. Deglaze the pan with a splash of the apple juice and scrape the pan contents into the soup pot. Add the pumpkin/garlic purée.

Add the remaining apple juice to the blender or food processor and purée, along with onion and apple sauté.

Add the onion-apple purée to the soup pot. Bring to a boil over medium-high heat and simmer gently for about 10–15 minutes.

To add the cream to the soup without curdling it, pull a cupful of hot soup out of the soup pot. Whisk the hot soup into the measured cream. Slowly add the soup/cream mixture back to the soup pot, stirring constantly. Do not let the soup return to a boil after this point, or the cream will curdle. (It's still fine to eat—it just won't look as nice.)

Continue cooking over low heat until very hot. If desired, thin soup with stock or apple juice.

Optional Garnishes

For an elegant touch, garnish with a swirl of roasted red pepper purée.

Sprinkle each serving with toasted, crushed cashews or roasted pumpkin seeds.

Come, ye thankful people, come
Raise the song of harvest-home!
All be safely gathered in,
Ere the winter storms begin;
God, our Maker, doth provide
For our wants to be supplied;
Come to God's own temple come,
Raise the song of harvest-home!
　　　　　—Thanksgiving Hymn

Hunterston Farm Squash with Orange & Ginger
serves 6

3 c water or stock
1 medium butternut squash
(roughly 3–4 # whole) OR
 any sweet squash, such as red kuri or delicata
1 head garlic (peel individual
cloves and leave whole)
2 T olive oil
1 yellow onion (peeled & chopped)
1 T fresh ginger (peeled & grated)
1 t ground cumin
1/2 t ground coriander
1/4 t cloves
1/4 t cinnamon
1/8 t cayenne (more, if desired)
Juice of 1 orange (about 1/2 c)
fresh lemon juice (optional)
salt & pepper to taste

Garnish with plain yogurt and fresh cilantro sprigs.

To make an easy stock for this soup, put all the seeds and strings from the squash, ginger peelings, orange halves and papery skin from the roasted garlic, along with 1 head of garlic (cloves separated, skins left on), 1 onion (unpeeled & quartered) and 1 potato (scrubbed & quartered) into a pot with 6 c water and 1 t salt. Bring to a boil, reduce heat and simmer for about an hour. Strain and discard the solids.

To roast squash: preheat the oven to 375ºF. Cut squash in half lengthwise. Remove seeds and strings with a spoon. Rub exposed flesh with some olive oil and sprinkle with salt and pepper. Toss whole garlic cloves with olive oil and place them in the empty squash halves. Place squash halves cut-side down on a lightly oiled roasting pan with sides. Roast until tender (when you can pierce the sides easily with a fork), about 30–40 minutes. Set aside until cool enough to handle. Scoop out flesh and purée, along with roasted cloves of garlic, in blender or food processor.

While squash is roasting, heat olive oil over medium heat in heavy pan. Add onion and 1/2 t salt and sauté until soft and translucent. Add ginger and spices and continue to sauté for another few minutes, adding a few splashes of stock or water to prevent sticking if necessary.

Place stock or water in a soup pot. Add orange juice and squash/garlic purée. Scrape sauté into soup pot, deglazing sauté pan with stock or water. Heat soup over medium-high heat until it begins to simmer, about 20 minutes. If desired, thin soup with stock or additional orange juice. Taste and adjust seasonings, adding more cayenne (if desired) and a bit of (optional) fresh lemon juice if the soup seems too sweet.

Variation
Sear 1/2 # mushrooms (see *Glossary* for instructions) and stir into soup pot about 5 minutes before serving.

Indonesian Coconut Curry Squash
serves 6

3 c stock or water
1 medium butternut squash
(roughly 3–4 # whole) OR
 any sweet squash, such as red kuri or delicata
2 T olive oil
1 yellow onion (peeled & diced)
1 T fresh ginger (peeled & grated)
1–2 serrano or jalapeño chilies
(remove seeds/membranes
 and mince OR mince with some
seeds for more heat)
1 t ground coriander
1 t ground cumin
1 t turmeric
1 T soy sauce or tamari
1 14-oz can coconut milk
1 bunch spinach (washed, trimmed
& cut into 1/2" ribbons)
juice of 1 lime

Garnish with plain yogurt and
thinly sliced green onions.

To make an easy stock for this soup, put all the seeds and strings from the squash and peelings from the ginger, along with 1 head of garlic (cloves separated, skins left on), 1 onion (unpeeled & quartered) and 1 potato (scrubbed & quartered) into a pot with 6 c water and 1 t salt. Bring to a boil, reduce heat and simmer for about an hour. Strain and discard the solids.

To roast squash: preheat the oven to 375ºF. Cut squash in half lengthwise. Remove seeds and strings with a spoon. Rub exposed flesh with some olive oil and sprinkle with salt and pepper. Toss whole garlic cloves with olive oil and place them in the empty squash halves. Place squash halves cut-side down on a lightly oiled roasting pan with sides. Roast until tender (when you can pierce the sides easily with a fork), about 30–40 minutes. Set aside until cool enough to handle. Scoop out flesh and purée, along with roasted cloves of garlic, in blender or food processor.

While squash is roasting, heat olive oil over medium heat in heavy pan. Add onion and 1/2 t salt and sauté until soft and translucent. Add ginger, chilies and spices and continue to sauté for another few minutes, adding a few splashes of stock or water to prevent sticking if necessary.

Place stock or water in a soup pot. Add coconut milk and squash/garlic purée. Scrape sauté into soup pot, deglazing sauté pan with soy sauce. Heat soup over medium-high heat until it begins to simmer, about 20 minutes. Don't let soup boil. If desired, thin soup with stock or water. Taste and adjust seasonings.

A minute or two before serving, add spinach ribbons and enough lime juice to sharpen (but not overpower) the flavors.

Optional Garnishes
Sprinkle each serving with toasted, chopped almonds or cashews.

Optional Additions

Add 1/2 c pitted, sliced green olives along with the spinach ribbons.

Add 1 bunch of fresh basil (washed, stemmed, leaves cut into thin ribbons) immediately before serving.

Reduce fresh garlic to 4 cloves; add 1 whole head of roasted garlic to the soup pot with the tomatoes.

Add the purée from 2 roasted red peppers (see *Some Basics* for instructions) to the soup pot with the tomatoes.

In the Lord, I'll be ever thankful.
In the Lord, I will rejoice.
Look to God, do not be afraid.
Lift up your voices, the Lord is near.
Lift up your voices, the Lord is near.
Amen.

–Taizé

the garden

All of us know that the water in which vegetables have been cooked contains valuable mineral matter. It hurts us to throw it out, but we do not want to serve it with the vegetables. The soup pot waits for such things, and in proportion as it receives them is the soup rich and tasty. Its success does not depend upon accurate measurements and specific ingredients but upon blended flavors.
—Claire de Pratz,
French Home Cooking

Summer Minestrone
serves 8

4–6 c water or stock
fresh thyme, rosemary and/or oregano sprigs (if available)
1 potato (scrubbed; cut into 1/2" cubes)
2 carrots (scrubbed; cut in half lengthwise, sliced crosswise)
2 stalks celery (sliced crosswise)
1 red pepper (seeds & stem removed; diced)
1 zucchini (unpeeled; cut in half lengthwise and sliced) OR
1 c beans (trimmed & cut in 1" pieces)
2 T olive oil
2 yellow onions (peeled & chopped)
6–8 cloves garlic (peeled & minced)
1 t dried leaf basil OR 1 T fresh, chopped
1 t dried leaf oregano OR 1 T fresh, chopped
1 t dried thyme OR 1 T fresh, chopped
1/2 c dry red wine (optional)
1–2 c cooked chick peas (use cooking water as stock) OR
 1 15-oz can, drained and rinsed chickpeas OR
 1–2 c fresh corn kernels, shaved off the cob
1 16-oz can crushed tomatoes + 1 T honey OR
1 # fresh tomatoes (peeled & seeded, puréed)
1 28-oz can whole tomatoes with juice (coarsely chopped)
 OR 2 # fresh tomatoes (peeled, seeded & chopped)

1/2 # pasta (any small shape; cooked separately)
1 bunch spinach (washed, stemmed, sliced into 1" ribbons)
Garnish with chopped fresh Italian parsley and grated Parmesan cheese.

Put stock or water in pot over medium-high heat. As you finish chopping each vegetable, add it to the stock. (Add potato first, then carrots, celery, red pepper and green beans.) *Note:* Zucchini will cook the fastest and doesn't need to be added until after the tomatoes.

While vegetables are cooking, heat olive oil over medium heat in heavy pan. Add onion and 1/2 t salt and sauté until onion is soft and translucent. Add garlic, basil, oregano and thyme and sauté for a couple more minutes. Add 1/4 c red wine and sauté until the liquid has been absorbed.

Transfer sauté to soup pot, deglazing the sauté pan with the rest of the red wine. Add the tomatoes (and honey if using canned), cooked chickpeas (or fresh corn) and zucchini, along with 1/4 t salt and some freshly ground pepper.

Once vegetables are just tender, taste and adjust seasonings. Add more honey if tomatoes are too acidic (an unmistakable metallic taste that comes from the can).

To make sure that the pasta doesn't absorb too much of the broth, cook it in a separate pot of boiling water and add it to the soup just before serving.

In the last 5 minutes, add the spinach ribbons and fresh herbs.

Winter Minestrone
serves 8

4–6 c water or stock
fresh rosemary sprigs (if available)
1 potato (scrubbed & cubed)
2 carrots (scrubbed; cut in half lengthwise; sliced crosswise)
1/2 head cauliflower (cut florets into pieces)
2 celery stalks (sliced crosswise)
1 bunch kale, chard or collards (washed, trimmed & sliced into 1/2" ribbons) OR 1 # Savoy cabbage (shredded)
2 T olive oil
1 yellow onion (peeled & chopped)
6–8 cloves garlic (peeled & minced)
1 t dried leaf basil
1 t dried leaf oregano
1 t dried thyme
2 leeks (white and tender green part only; cut in half lengthwise; washed well; sliced crosswise)
1/2 c red or white wine
1 15-oz can crushed tomatoes + 2 t honey
1 28-oz can whole tomatoes with juice (coarsely chopped)
1–2 c cooked chick peas OR cranberry beans (include the cooking water in the stock) OR
1 15-oz can chickpeas OR cranberry beans (drained & rinsed well)

1 bunch broccoli (florets cut into pieces; stalk peeled, diced)
1/2 # pasta (any small shape; cooked separately)
Garnish with grated Parmesan cheese.

Put stock or water in pot over medium-high heat with fresh rosemary. As you finish chopping each vegetable, add it to the stock. (Add potato first, then carrots, cauliflower, celery, and kale or collards. Broccoli, chard and cabbage will cook faster and do not need to be added until later.)

While vegetables are cooking, heat olive oil over medium heat in heavy pan. Add onion, 1/2 t salt, basil and oregano. When onion is soft, add garlic and thyme. Continue to sauté until onion is translucent. Add leeks and sauté for another couple minutes. Then add 1/4 c white wine and sauté until the liquid has been absorbed.

Add sauté to soup pot, deglazing the sauté pan with the rest of the white wine. Add tomatoes (and honey), cooked chickpeas (or cranberry beans) and broccoli to the soup pot, along with 1/4 t salt and some freshly ground pepper.

Once vegetables are just tender, taste and adjust seasonings. Add more honey if tomatoes are too acidic (an unmistakable metallic taste that comes from the can).

To make sure that the pasta doesn't absorb the broth, cook it in a separate pot of boiling water and add it to the soup before serving.

In the last 5–10 minutes, add the chard ribbons or shredded cabbage (if using).

Note: Winter (or summer) minestrone is delicious the next day, but you will need to add additional stock, water or tomato purée to thin the soup, as the pasta will absorb the broth. To avoid this, add the cooked pasta to each bowl before serving.

Optional Additions

Reduce fresh garlic to 4 cloves; add 1 whole head of roasted garlic to the soup pot with the tomatoes.

Add the purée from 2 roasted red peppers (see *Some Basics* for instructions) to the soup pot with the tomatoes.

Live in each season as it passes; breathe the air, drink the drink, taste the fruit, and resign yourself to the influence of each. Grow green with spring, yellow and ripe with autumn.
—Henry David Thoreau

*Soup sought is good,
but given unsought is better.*
—Old Proverb

A Weekend around the Wilkinson's Table

Breakfast
    Dutch Babies   57
    Crêpes   58
    Waffles   58
    Cinnamon Buns   59

Pastas & Sauces
    Artichoke Heart Pasta   60
    Pesto   60
    Peruvian Sauce   61
    Spaghetti Sauce   61

Soup, Salad & Bread
    Tomato Soup   62
    Boatman's Stew   62
    Butternut Squash Soup   63
    Caesar Salad   63
    Cheesy Flat Bread   64

Sweet Delights
    Apple Pie   65
    Maple Walnut Pie   66
    Erik's Cookie Bars   66
    Really Good Chocolate Chip Cookies   67
    Russian Teas   67

Big Dutch Babies

makes 3–6 servings

Based on the size of pan you're going to use, figure ingredients based on this chart:

Pan Size	Butter	Eggs	Milk & Flour
2–3 qt	1/4 c	3	3/4 c each
3–4 qt	1/3 c	4	1 c each
4–4 1/2 qt	1/2 c	5	1 1/4 c each
4 1/2–5 qt	1/2 c	6	1 1/2 c each

Place butter in pan and set in a 425°F oven. While butter melts, mix batter quickly. Put eggs in a blender or food processor and whirl at high speed for 1 minute. With motor running, gradually pour in milk, then slowly add flour; continue whirling for 30 seconds. Or, in a bowl, beat eggs until blended; gradually beat in milk, then flour.

Remove pan from oven and pour in batter. Return pan to oven and bake until pancake is puffy and well browned (20–25 minutes, depending on pan size).

Dust pancake with ground nutmeg, if you wish. Cut in wedges and serve at once with any of the following toppings.

Powdered sugar classic: Have a shaker or bowl of powdered sugar and thick wedges of lemon at the table. Sprinkle sugar on hot pancake, then squeeze on lemon juice.

Fruit: Sliced strawberries or peaches, sweetened to taste, or any fruits in season, cut and sweetened. Or substitute canned or frozen fruit.

Hot fruit: Glazed apples or pears make a good toping; offer with sour cream or yogurt. Or heat banana or papaya slices in melted butter or margarine over medium heat, turning until hot; serve with lime wedges.

Canned pie filling: To cherry or apple pie filling, add lemon juice and ground cinnamon to taste. Serve cold or warm, topped with yogurt or sour cream.

Syrups: Serve with warm or room temperature honey, maple syrup, or any favorite fruit sauce.

Crêpes

serves 4–5

1 1/2 c flour
salt and sugar to taste (roughly 1/2 t salt and 2 T sugar)
2 c milk
6 eggs

Mix everything in a blender or food processor (should be smooth).

Pour just enough in hot greased skillet or crêpe pan to cover the bottom of pan (tilt and rotate the pan or skillet a bit).

These keep well in a low oven stacked and covered with a slightly damp cloth.

Serve with sweet or savory toppings.

Waffles

3 c flour
5 t baking powder
1 t salt
2 T sugar
2 2/3 c milk
2/3 c cooking oil
6 eggs

Mix dry ingredients in a large bowl.

Make a well in the center of the dry ingredients and add wet ingredients. Stir with a fork to break the egg yolks; gradually include dry ingredients. Don't over-mix. Waffle batter should be a bit lumpy. For lighter waffles, separate the eggs. Whip the whites till stiff and add to the mixed batter.

Bake on hot, greased waffle iron.

Cinnamon Buns
makes 16 buns

Mix following together in a large bowl:
    1/4 c sugar
    3/4 c cut margarine
    1/2 t salt
    1 c boiling water (or just *very* hot tap water)

In a separate bowl, mix together following:
    1/2 c lukewarm water
    2 T yeast
    1/4 c sugar
    Let sit until it bubbles, about 10 minutes.

When sugar and margarine mixture is lukewarm, stir in yeast mixture. Then add:
    2 beaten eggs
    3 c flour
    1/2 c oats
Beat well. Then add:
    1 c flour
Beat again.

Let rise until doubled (45 minutes or less). Turn out on heavily floured board and knead a bit. Roll out to 18" x 24" rectangle.

Spread dough with very thin coating of melted butter. Cover with ground cinnamon till all brown. Sprinkle evenly with a very small amount of brown sugar.

Roll up from wide side; pinch edges. Cut in half. Cut halves in half. Cut fourths in half. (We're trying to get 16 buns here.) Put 8 buns in each of 2 greased pie or cake pans.

Cook at 375°F for at least 20 minutes until just browned. Let sit a moment after removing from oven.

To make icing, mix the following in a bowl:
    1–1 1/2 c icing sugar
    finely grated orange rind
    2 t vanilla
    1 T melted butter
    enough cream or milk to make
    the mixture spreadable

Artichoke Heart Pasta
serves 4

    2 T butter
    3 cloves garlic, minced
    1 can (not marinated) artichoke hearts, drained and cut in
     sixths
    1/2 c wine
    1 c heavy cream
    1 T dried parsley
    1 # cooked noodles (linguini)
    coarse black pepper
    grated Parmesan cheese

Melt butter in frying pan. Lightly sauté garlic. Add artichoke hearts and wine. Bring to boil. Add heavy cream and let bubble. Remove from heat, add parsley and pepper. Add noodles and cheese.

Pesto

We have used very differing proportions of these ingredients, and it always seems to turn out okay. Here's a rough estimate:

    2 c basil (fresh or frozen)
    1 c walnuts (cheaper than pine nuts and just as "Italian")
    2–3 heads (at least 20 cloves) garlic (the key ingredient)
    grated Parmesan cheese
    olive oil
    I often add some parsley too, which we can get fresh year-
     round.

Purée in a food processor. Add enough olive oil to give the texture you want.

This will keep for at least two weeks in the refrigerator in a sealed container.

Peruvian Sauce
makes about 6 pints

    4 qt, or about 24 large, red-ripe tomatoes (peeled, cored, chopped)
    1 qt chopped onions
    1 qt, or about 4–5 medium, apples (chopped, cored, pared)
    1 1/2 c, or about 3 medium, sweet green peppers (chopped)
    1 hot red pepper
    1 head garlic, crushed
    3 c brown sugar, packed
    1 T salt
    2 T ground allspice
    2 T mustard seed
    2 t ground cinnamon
    3 c vinegar

Combine tomatoes, onions, apples, peppers, garlic and sugar. Cook slowly until thick, about 1 hour. As mixture thickens, stir frequently to prevent sticking. Add salt, spices and vinegar. Cook until thick as wanted, 45–60 minutes. Pour, boiling hot, into sterilized (in 225° oven for 20 min) Ball jars, leaving 1/8" head space. Adjust caps.

Spaghetti Sauce
serves 20

In a large, heavy-bottomed pan, sauté 3–4 medium onions in olive oil; add up to one head of garlic, crushed or chopped.

Brown a couple of pounds of hamburger (add a bit of sausage or bacon if you like), taking care not to burn the onion.

Add 4 quarts of chopped tomatoes and a cup or two of tomato paste. Add herbs and spices, especially rosemary, oregano (or any good mix of Italian seasonings), hot pepper and salt, to taste.

I often add some chopped green peppers for both colour and flavour.

Add about a cup of red wine.

Simmer slowly with the lid off for several hours; put lid on when the sauce reaches desired consistency, but keep simmering.

Tomato Soup

Basic:
2 c tomatoes
1/2 c chopped celery
1/4 c chopped onion
2 T brown sugar

Cream sauce:
4 T butter
4 T flour
2 c milk

Make it tasty:
Salt & pepper
Parsley
Hot Peppers
Marjoram
Tarragon

Boatman's Stew

2 # fish (cod is good)
3/4 t salt
2 large onions, sliced
1/2 T olive oil
1 big can tomatoes
1 8-oz. can tomato sauce
1 t crushed red pepper
salt & pepper to taste
1 t marjoram
1/2 bunch parsley
1/2 c white wine
1 1/2 c water or beef bullion

Cut up and salt fish awhile. Sauté onions in oil until beginning to brown. Add all ingredients but fish and simmer for 30 minutes. Add fish, don't stir much. Serve over cubed cheese and bread.

Butternut Squash Soup
serves 16

You will need 6–8 pounds of cooked butternut squash, so start with 8–10 pounds of uncooked squash. Slice them longitudinally; place in a baking pan and put about an inch of water in the pan. Cook for about an hour at 350ºF.

Cool, and scrape out the squash.

In a large soup pot, sauté 4 or 5 medium chopped onions in a generous amount of olive oil; crush or chop one head of garlic and sauté it as well.

Add about 24 c of stock (we use juice from our canned beans and supplement with vegetable bullion). Any good soup stock will work.

Add the baked squash; chop a handful of fresh rosemary and add it; add the grated peel of one orange and the juice of one or two oranges.

Blend with an electric hand blender (you might be able to skip this step, but it makes the soup nice and smooth.)

Add salt to taste; heat. I usually add a bit more chopped rosemary and chopped dried tomatoes for color and taste. Unlike many soups, this doesn't seem to gain much from long cooking, so it can be put together very quickly.

I have sometimes added a little maple syrup or apple cider in place of orange juice. Also a bit of hot red pepper. Tom has a good curry version. Experiment.

Caesar Salad
dresses 1 medium head of Romaine

6 T olive oil
4 T lemon juice
2–3 squirts Worcestershire sauce
1 t salt
1/2 t garlic powder or 1 garlic clove
1/4 t dry mustard
1 hardboiled egg
1/4 c Parmesan cheese
4 strips bacon, fried crisp and crumbled

Combine everything except egg and pour over Romaine lettuce. Cube egg and top salad just before serving.

Cheesy Flat Bread
makes 2 (9") pie pans

Bread:
1 3/4 c warm water
1 T sugar
1 T yeast
2 T oil
1 1/2 t salt
1/4 c milk powder
about 2 1/2 c flour (+ enough unbleached flour to make thick but stir-able mixture)

Mix water, sugar and yeast. Let come to a bubble (about 10 minutes).

Add oil, salt, milk powder and flour into yeast mixture and stir for 150 beats. Add enough additional flour to make a very soft dough. Let rise 45 minutes.

Topping:
3 T onion (or a little more)
1/4 c melted butter
1/2 t paprika
1/2 t oregano (or a little more)
1/4 t celery salt
1/4 t garlic salt

Combine all ingredients in saucepan and cook a little.

Put bread dough into pie pans. Spread with topping. Sprinkle bread with 1–1 1/2 cups shredded cheddar cheese. Prick generously with a fork. Let rise 30 minutes or less (or not at all!)

Bake at 375°F for 20–25 minutes.

Apple Pie

Filling:
3 qt, or about 6–7, apples (peeled, pared, cored, sliced)
1 t ground cinnamon
1/2 t ground cloves
1/4 c flour
1 c sugar
Mix together in 3 qt mixing bowl

Crust:
2 c flour
1 t salt
3/4 c cheap hard margarine (not the tub type; canola oil margarine is my favorite)
1 c of ice cold water (or cold from the tap)

Add flour, salt and margarine. With fingers break down margarine till pea sized. Add cold water a little at a time, stirring till mixture clumps. The dough should not be crumbly, but not be sticky either. Stir as little as possible! Divide in half and roll out bottom crust and put in pie pan. Put in pie filling, pressing down as you go & being careful not to puncture crust. Dot apples with 1 to 2 tbs of bits of butter. Roll out top crust and lay over apples. Fold the top edge under bottom edge & crimp edges with fingers.

Cut a pattern in the top crust. The pattern and the edge are your personal "signature." Whisk an egg and brush over top crust.

Bake at 375°F for about 1 hour. You may need to turn down the temperature towards the end. A fork stuck through the cut should meet with softened apples.

Maple Walnut Pie

1 (9") unbaked pie crust
1/2 c brown sugar
2 T all-purpose flour
1 1/4 c maple syrup
3 T butter
1/4 t salt
3 eggs
1 1/2 t maple flavored extract
1 c walnut halves

Preheat oven to 375°F. In a saucepan, mix brown sugar and flour. Add maple syrup, butter and salt. Heat until butter melts, stirring constantly. In a medium bowl, beat eggs with maple flavoring. Stir in sugar mixture. Pour into unbaked pie shell and sprinkle with walnuts. Bake in the preheated oven for 40 to 45 minutes, or until filling is set.

Erik's Cookie Bars

1 c shortening
3 c or less brown sugar
3 eggs
3 t vanilla
3 c flour
3/4 t baking soda
3/4 t salt
1 large package chocolate chips
1 c chopped nuts or coconut

Blend shortening and brown sugar to a cream. Add vanilla and eggs and beat well. Add flour, baking soda and salt and mix well. Add chocolate chips and optional nuts. Spread in greased jellyroll pan. Bake at 350°F for 25–30 minutes.

Really Good Chocolate Chip Cookies

1 c butter (not margarine)
1 c brown sugar
1 egg
1/2 t vanilla
2 c flour
1/2 t salt
1 c chocolate chips

Put all in mixer. Mix. Drop onto cookie sheets. Bake at 350° until done.

Russian Tea

2 sticks cinnamon
2 (or more) whole cloves
2 c cold water
1 teabag
2 c (or less) sugar
2 c orange juice
1/2 c fresh lemon juice
8–10 c water

Bring 2 c water, cinnamon and cloves to boil. Add teabag and steep for 10 minutes. Strain out spices. Combine sugar, orange juice, lemon juice and rest of water. Heat and serve.